Mexico's A City

Guadalajara

(Travel Guide)

Rex Egah

Contents

Chapter 1: Introduction 8

Brief Overview of Guadalajara 8

The Importance of a Comprehensive Travel
Guide 9

History and Culture: Unveiling the Rich
Tapestry of Guadalajara 10

Historical Significance: Tracing Guadalajara's
Roots 10

Cultural Heritage: Where Tradition Meets
Modernity 11

Influential Figures: Icons of Guadalajara's
Legacy 11

Chapter 2: Navigating the City with a Smile 13

Transportation Tango Public Transport
Options 13

Unveiling the Heart of Mexico's
Neighborhoods and Districts 15

Zapopan: The City of Eternal Spring 16

Tonala: Craftsmanship Unveiled 18

Chapter 3: Must-See Attractions for Fun-
Loving Tourists 20

Guadalajara Cathedral - A Marvel of
Architectural Beauty 21

Hospicio Cabañas - Where Art and History
Dance Together 22

Rotonda de los Jaliscienses Ilustres - Honoring Jalisco's Heroes 23

Guadalajara's most interesting museums and galleries! 25

Instituto Cultural Cabañas - Where Art Meets History 25

Museo Regional de Guadalajara - A Glimpse into Jalisco's Past 26

Museo de las Artes Universidad de Guadalajara - Where Modernity Meets Creativity 26

Museo Regional de Guadalajara: A Step Back in Time..27

Museo de las Artes Universidad de Guadalajara: The Playground of Creativity 28

Chapter 4: Embracing Nature in Guadalajara 29

Parque Metropolitano: Where Nature Meets Adventure...30

Bosque Los Colomos: Where Elegance Meets Nature's Bounty 31

Plaza Tapatía: Where Culture and Greenery..32

Chapter 5: Experiencing Guadalajara's Culture: A Culinary Adventure 33

Birria: 34

Tortas Ahogadas: 35

Pozole: 36

Notable Restaurants and Eateries: Where Every Bite is a Standing Ovation 37

Street Food Experiences: Where Every Corner Holds a Culinary Treasure 38

Elotes and Esquites 39

Tacos al Pastor 40

Churros and Champurrado 41

Chapter 6: Guadalajara: Where Arts and Entertainment Get the Party Started! 42

Theatres & Performance Venues: Where Drama Meets Fiesta 42

Street Art and Murals: Where Walls Tell Stories 44

Music Scene and Festivals: Where Every Beat is a Celebration 45

Chapter 7: Immersive Experiences: Dive Headfirst into Guadalajara's Charm 47

Language & Communication: Speak Like a True Tapatío 48

Language Schools or Resources: Where Learning Feels Like a Fiesta 49

Fun and Learning in Guadalajara: Workshops That'll Make You Feel Like a Pro 51

Traditional Crafts and Skills: Unleash Your Inner Artisan 51

Cooking Classes: Turn Up the Heat in the Kitchen 53

Dance & Music Lessons: Move and Groove Like a Local 54

Guadalajara's Fiesta Extravaganza: Where Every Day is a Celebration! 55

Overview of Major Festivals: Let the Good Times Roll! 55

Dates and Locations: Where the Party's At! ...56

Unique Traditions: The Quirks That Make Guadalajara Special 57

Chapter 8: Day Trips & Excursions: Unleashing the Fun Around Guadalajara! 59

Destinations Near Guadalajara: Where Magic Awaits..60

Tlaquepaque: The Artistic Wonderland 60

Tequila: Where the Spirit Comes Alive...........61

Chapala: Lakeside Serenity 62

Transportation Options for Day Trips: Getting There in Style 63

Recommended Itineraries: Making the Most of Your Day 64

Safety Tips: Where Fun Meets Safety.......66

General Safety Advice: Navigating Guadalajara like a Pro 66

Chapter 9: More Pro Tips to keep you Safe .68

Emergency Contacts: Your Safety Squad 68

Guadalajara's Healthy Hubs: Where Care Comes with a Dash of Cheer 70

Hospitals and Clinics: Where Healing Meets Hilarity 70

Pharmacies and Medical Services: More Smiles, Less Stress 71

Chapter 10: Staying Connected in Guadalajara: SIM Cards, Wi-Fi, and Communication Shenanigans 73

SIM Cards and Internet Access: Unleashing Your Inner Tech Wizard 74

Wi-Fi Wonderland: Where to Find Your Digital Oasis 75

Parks: Nature and Net Neutrality 76

Co-Working Spaces: Where Work Meets Play 76

Conclusion: Where Every Corner Holds a Fiesta! 78

Maps 81

Chapter 1 : Introduction

Guadalajara! The country of mariachi music, delectable tacos, and of course, the origin of tequila. If you're planning a vacation to this bustling Mexican city, you're in for a treat. But hang on tight, because I'm going to offer you the ultimate insider's guide that will make your experience memorable.

Brief Overview of Guadalajara

Nestled in the heart of Jalisco, Guadalajara is Mexico's second-largest city and a treasure mine of culture, history, and gastronomic pleasures. From its quaint cobblestone alleys to its vibrant plazas, this city radiates life and emits warmth that's impossible to resist.

The Importance of a Comprehensive Travel Guide

Now, you may ask why you need a complete travel guide when you can simply wing it. Well, my fellow traveler, although spontaneity has its appeal, Guadalajara is a city brimming with so much to see and do that you'd be silly not to have a game plan.

History and Culture: Unveiling the Rich Tapestry of Guadalajara

Guadalajara, the dynamic hub of Jalisco, Mexico, is a city rich in history and culture. From its cobblestone alleys to its vibrant plazas, every nook emanates the spirit of Mexican history. Let's begin on a trip to explore the historical importance and cultural treasures of this wonderful city.

Historical Significance: Tracing Guadalajara's Roots

Guadalajara's history extends back to the early 16th century when it was established by Spanish conquistadors. Explore the architectural treasures of the city's historic core, where colonial buildings remain as living testaments to a bygone age. Walk in the footsteps of history and observe the combination of Spanish and Mesoamerican influences that create Guadalajara's character.

Cultural Heritage: Where Tradition Meets Modernity

The heart of Guadalajara pulses with the rhythm of mariachi music, a genre developed on these exact streets. Immerse yourself in the colorful ambiance of Plaza de los Mariachis, where brilliant musicians entertain guests with soul-stirring tunes. Beyond music, Guadalajara features a flourishing arts culture, with galleries and museums presenting both traditional and modern Mexican art.

Influential Figures: Icons of Guadalajara's Legacy

Guadalajara has been the birthplace of many notable personalities who have left an unmistakable effect on Mexican history. Visit the childhood home of famed muralist Jose Clemente Orozco, whose evocative artwork depicts themes of hardship and victory. Stroll around the parks and squares named for heroes like Miguel Hidalgo, heroes who played crucial roles in Mexico's war for independence.

Chapter 2: Navigating the City with a Smile

Navigating a new place can be both exhilarating and daunting. In Guadalajara, Mexico's lively cultural metropolis, getting around is an experience in itself. This part of our travel guide is meant to help you sail through the city with a bit of humor and a friendly push.

Transportation Tango Public Transport Options

Guadalajara provides a selection of public transit alternatives that are not only efficient but also pocket-friendly. The lifeblood of the city's transportation system is its massive bus network. Jump aboard a 'Macrobus' for a quick tour of the city or choose for a 'Tren Ligero' for a more relaxing tram experience.

Renting a Car: To Zoom or Not to Zoom? Renting a vehicle in Guadalajara may be freeing, particularly if you're hoping to visit neighboring sites like the lovely Lake Chapala or the scenic town of Tequila. Just remember, the streets may be a bit of a labyrinth, and traffic can become hectic. But hey, it's all part of the Guadalajara experience!

Taxi Services: The Talkative Drivers
If you're eager for some local chitchat, catching a cab is a terrific way to navigate about Guadalajara. The drivers here are noted for their cheerful disposition and, well, their readiness to tell a tale or two. It's like having your own personal tour guide, with a sprinkling of good-natured humor.

Unveiling the Heart of Mexico's Neighborhoods and Districts

Guadalajara, frequently referred to as the "Pearl of the West," is a dynamic city that features a rich cultural legacy, exquisite food, and a lively environment. As you commence on your tour through this Mexican treasure, let's traverse the city via its varied neighborhoods and districts, each giving a distinct experience.

Chapultepec:

Where Tradition Meets Trend
Nestled in the center of the city,
Chapultepec is an area that easily mixes

heritage with contemporary. It's famed for its tree-lined roads, lively markets, and a selection of quaint cafés. Take a leisurely walk down Avenida Chapultepec and immerse yourself in the creative aura that pervades this region.

Zapopan: The City of Eternal Spring

Located to the northwest of Guadalajara's core, Zapopan greets you with its mild atmosphere and lovely streets. The medieval Basilica of Zapopan is a must-visit, affording a look into the city's religious legacy. Explore the bustling marketplaces and sample local specialities as you absorb in the laid-back environment.

Accommodation Options in Zapopan
Hotel Real Zapopan:
A combination of comfort and elegance, offers an accessible location.
Hacienda del Sol: A peaceful getaway with magnificent landscapes and contemporary conveniences.
Tlaquepaque: Artisanal Haven
For a taste of creative flare, travel to Tlaquepaque, a neighborhood famed for its handmade treasures and active arts scene. Cobblestone streets take you to colorful workshops and galleries where you may observe craftspeople at work. Don't miss out on discovering El Parian, a lively area packed with music, dancing, and local cuisine.

Tonala: Craftsmanship Unveiled

Known as the artisan city of Guadalajara, Tonala is a treasure trove of ceramics, glassware, and textiles. The lively markets provide a selection of handcrafted products, making it the ideal spot to pick up mementos. Engage with local craftspeople, and observe the meticulous process behind these creations.

Accommodation Choices in Tonala Casa de las Flores: A comfortable bed-and-breakfast with a friendly environment.

Hotel Mi Pueblito: A pleasant overnight choice with convenient access to Tonala's bustling markets.

Chapter 3: Must-See Attractions for Fun-Loving Tourists

As a seasoned traveler, I can promise you that this city is rich with charm, history, and an infectious sense of fun. Join me on this lovely excursion as we see the must-see sights, including some of the most recognizable historic landmarks.

Guadalajara Cathedral - A Marvel of Architectural Beauty

Nestled in the heart of Guadalajara's historic center, the Guadalajara Cathedral rises towering, a tribute to the city's rich past. Its magnificent neo-gothic exterior and detailed detailing are a photographer's delight.

Step inside, and you'll be welcomed with awe-inspiring architecture, vibrant stained glass windows, and magnificent altars. The combination of light and shadow produces a captivating ambiance that genuinely captivates the spirit.

For a panoramic perspective of the city, ascend the bell tower. The hike is worth every step, affording a stunning sight of Guadalajara's skyline.

Hospicio Cabañas - Where Art and History Dance Together

Hospicio Cabañas, a UNESCO World Heritage Site, is a cultural treasure trove. Originally an orphanage, its vast courtyards and beautiful paintings by José Clemente Orozco make it a must-visit.

As you travel around the hallways, Orozco's paintings will take you to a realm of intense emotion and social insight. The sheer scope and intensity of his art are guaranteed to leave you in awe.

Take your time wandering the courtyards, where the play of light and shadows intensifies the splendor of this medieval jewel. It's a fantastic area to relax and enjoy the creative ambience.

Rotonda de los Jaliscienses Ilustres - Honoring Jalisco's Heroes

This circular monument pays respect to the famous individuals of Jalisco, from artists to revolutionaries. The monuments stand tall, each presenting a narrative of bravery, ingenuity, and endurance.

As you go around the Rotonda, you'll get a feeling of pride and inspiration. It's a location where history comes to life, and you can't help but think of the achievements of these extraordinary people.

Guadalajara's most interesting museums and galleries!

Instituto Cultural Cabañas - Where Art Meets History

Tucked away in the heart of Guadalajara, Instituto Cultural Cabañas is a treasure trove of creative delights. Imagine entering into a world where paintings come alive, each conveying a narrative of Mexico's rich past. As a visitor, you'll find yourself enveloped in the awe-inspiring paintings of Orozco, a famous Mexican muralist. The creative mix of colors and patterns will leave you fascinated.

Museo Regional de Guadalajara - A Glimpse into Jalisco's Past

Have you ever longed to step back in time? Well, Museo Regional de Guadalajara takes you on a tour through the chronicles of Jalisco's history. Stroll through the hallways packed with antiques and displays that bring to life the traditions and legacy of this lovely area. From pre-Columbian antiques to colonial-era gems, this museum is a time machine you won't want to miss.

Museo de las Artes Universidad de Guadalajara - Where Modernity Meets Creativity

Guadalajara isn't only about history—it's a vibrant center of modern art too! At Museo de las Artes, creativity has no limitations. You'll find yourself immersed in a world of avant-garde installations, thought-provoking exhibitions, and interactive displays. It's a monument to the city's lively creative energy.

Museo Regional de Guadalajara: A Step Back in Time

Have you ever thought of wearing a tricorn hat and wandering through the annals of history? Well, Museo Regional de Guadalajara is the closest you'll get! This museum is a treasure trove of Jalisco's history, where each exhibit is a glimpse into a bygone period. From pre-Columbian treasures to colonial-era antiques, every piece tells a narrative of the people who formed this place. It's like a live, breathing history book, and you get to flip the pages.

Museo de las Artes Universidad de Guadalajara: The Playground of Creativity

Modernity meets creativity at Museo de las Artes. As you enter inside, you're confronted with a tornado of avant-garde works, each more intriguing than the last. This museum isn't simply a place to view; it's an invitation to connect with art in ways you never imagined possible. The displays challenge your viewpoint and inspire your creativity. It's a monument to Guadalajara's vibrant creative energy, where history and innovation dance hand in hand.

Chapter 4: Embracing Nature in Guadalajara

Nestled in the heart of Mexico, Guadalajara is a city of lively culture, rich history, and beautiful natural beauty. While touring this vibrant city, don't forget to take a break in its beautiful parks and green areas. In this chapter, we'll introduce you to three of the loveliest green oasis in Guadalajara.

Parque Metropolitano: Where Nature Meets Adventure

A Glimpse into Parque Metropolitano

Parque Metropolitano, frequently termed the "lung of Guadalajara," is an immense haven for wildlife aficionados. With over 600 acres of lush vegetation, this park provides a refuge for leisure and pleasure.

For the thrill-seekers, Parque Metropolitano doesn't disappoint. Zip line over the trees or starting on a hard walk up Cerro de la Reina are just some of the amazing things you may experience.

If you want a more calm experience, take a picnic and choose a nice location near one of the beautiful ponds. Take a leisurely walk around the meandering trails, and you could even see some of the park's local species.

Bosque Los Colomos: Where Elegance Meets Nature's Bounty

Unveiling Bosque Los Colomos
Bosque Los Colomos is a monument to the perfect coexistence of art and environment. This park is recognised for its beautifully maintained gardens, vast meadows, and tranquil lakes.

One of the features of Bosque Los Colomos is its gorgeous botanical garden, presenting a rainbow of plants from throughout the globe. A leisurely walk through this bright garden is like entering into a living artwork. Bosque Los Colomos boasts an aura of refined elegance, making it a great setting for a relaxing day. Find a seat in the shade of a big tree and bury yourself in a good book, or just absorb in the tranquil environment.

Plaza Tapatía: Where Culture and Greenery

Plaza Tapatía is not only a park; it's a cultural tapestry stitched with threads of history, art, and nature. This enormous area is a center of activity and a tribute to Guadalajara's dynamic personality. As you travel around Plaza Tapatía, you'll see a collection of artworks and installations, beautifully incorporated into the lush green surroundings. It's a tribute to the city's devotion to blending art with nature.

Plaza Tapatía regularly holds colorful events and concerts, giving an added dimension of excitement to your visit. Keep a watch out for local artists and musicians, whose abilities infuse life into this colorful area.

Chapter 5: Experiencing Guadalajara's Culture: A Culinary Adventure

Traditional Dishes: Where Flavor Takes Center Stage

Alright, guys, saddle up your taste buds because we're delving into the heart and soul of Guadalajara's culture - its cuisine! This isn't just ordinary food; it's a symphony of sensations that'll have your taste buds dancing a cha-cha-cha.

Birria:

Picture this - luscious, slow-cooked beef, oozing with flavor, served with a dish of creamy, spicy consommé. It's the type of food that makes you want to hug the cook!

Tortas Ahogadas:

These sandwiches are like the rockstars of the street food industry. Soft, crusty bread, packed with succulent pork and drowned in a zesty tomato sauce. Messy? Absolutely. Worth every exquisite bite? You bet!

Pozole:

This rich soup is like a warm, loving embrace from abuelita. It's got hominy, succulent bits of pork, and a broth that's been simmering to perfection. Top it with radishes, lime, and a sprinkling of crispy tostadas for the whole experience.

Notable Restaurants and Eateries: Where Every Bite is a Standing Ovation

Now, let's speak about the areas where these gastronomic masterpieces come to life. These aren't simply restaurants; they're stages where the cooks are the maestros, and every meal is a masterpiece.

La Chata: Imagine coming into a setting where tradition meets contemporary, and every meal tells a tale. La Chata is where you'll discover the classics served with a touch of modern flare.

Hueso: If you've ever wondered what eating within a jaw-dropping art exhibit might feel like, wonder no more. At Hueso, you'll find yourself surrounded by a magnificent skeleton design while eating some of the most innovative meals in town.

Karne Garibaldi: Here, speed meets taste in the most wonderful manner conceivable. Known for boasting the world's quickest waiters, this eatery is all about dishing you scalding hot, exquisite food at breakneck speed.

Street Food Experiences: Where Every Corner Holds a Culinary Treasure

Now, let's hit the streets, shall we? Guadalajara's street food culture is like a carnival for your taste buds - bright, energetic, and absolutely enticing.

Elotes and Esquites

Imagine luscious, juicy corn on a stick, slathered with mayo, cheese, and chili powder. That's elotes for you. And if you want it off the cob, esquites is your jam – a cup full of corny delight!

Tacos al Pastor

These tacos are like a party in your mouth. Thin slices of marinated pork, grilled to perfection, topped with pineapple, then wrapped between a warm tortilla. It's a taste explosion you won't soon forget.

Churros and Champurrado

Wrap off your gastronomic excursion with a delicious finale. Sink your teeth into a crispy, cinnamon-dusted churro, then wash it down with a cup of champurrado - a rich, chocolaty drink that's like a warm embrace for your taste buds.

Chapter 6: Guadalajara: Where Arts and Entertainment Get the Party Started!

Theatres & Performance Venues: Where Drama Meets Fiesta

Alright, theater enthusiasts and party freaks, listen up! Guadalajara is where the stage comes alive with drama, humor, and everything in between.

Teatro Degollado: Picture this - elegant balconies, rich crimson draperies, and a chandelier that'll make your mouth drop. That's Teatro Degollado for you. It's like walking into a scene from a royal ball, but with a dash of Mexican flare.

Foro Independencia: This location is like the hip cousin of the theatrical world. It's tiny, it's edgy, and it's where you'll witness the newest in indie performances, from experimental plays to live music events that'll have you dancing in your seat.

Conjunto de Artes Escénicas: If you're searching for a cultural powerhouse, this is it. It's got everything - opera, ballet, theater, you name it. Plus, the building is so futuristic and elegant, you'll feel like you've walked into the future.

Street Art and Murals: Where Walls Tell Stories

Now, let's discuss the dynamic realm of street art. Guadalajara's streets are like a canvas, and every mural tells a narrative.

Barrio de las 9 Esquinas: This area is like an outdoor art exhibit. Every time you turn, there's a fresh piece of art ready to enchant you. From vibrant, larger-than-life murals to detailed, thought-provoking patterns, it's a visual feast.

Calzada de los Héroes: This boulevard is like a tour through an open-air museum. The walls are covered with paintings representing the rich history and culture of Mexico. It's like receiving a crash lesson in art and history, but a lot more fun!

Mercado de San Juan de Dios: Even the marketplaces of Guadalajara are brimming with artistic flare. Take a trip through this maze of booths, and you'll find yourself surrounded by vivid murals that provide a burst of color to your shopping binge.

Music Scene and Festivals: Where Every Beat is a Celebration

Alright, music lovers, get ready to get your socks knocked off because Guadalajara knows how to throw a party!

Festival Internacional de Mariachi: This is the mother of all mariachi celebrations. Picture hundreds of musicians in their charro attire, serenading the masses with soul-stirring sounds. It's a musical spectacular that'll have you clapping your feet and singing along.

Festival Internacional de Cine en Guadalajara: It's not just about music – Guadalajara likes its flicks too! This festival brings together filmmakers from all around the globe, showing anything from thought-provoking documentaries to edge-of-your-seat thrillers.

Rojo Café Concert Hall: This venue is where you go for a taste of live music with your morning coffee. It's quiet, it's intimate, and it's where local artists congregate to serenade you with their heartfelt sounds.

Chapter 7: Immersive Experiences: Dive Headfirst into Guadalajara's Charm

If you're here to soak up the local atmosphere, you're in for a treat.

Mariachi Serenades: Picture this: You, surrounded by a band of happy mariachis, singing out melodies that make your heart sing. That's a Guadalajara classic, buddies!

Artisan Workshops in Tlaquepaque: Ever longed to construct your own masterpiece? Tlaquepaque's artisan workshops have got you covered. From pottery to glassblowing, unleash your inner creativity!

Lucha Libre Nights: Grab a mask and get ready for some high-flying, body-slamming action. Lucha Libre evenings are like no other - a crazy spectacle that'll have you shouting for more!

Language & Communication: Speak Like a True Tapatío

So, you've chosen to plunge into the local lingo? ¡Muy bien! Here are some simple Spanish phrases to get you started on your language journey:

- **Hola** (Oh-la): Hello! Use this to brighten anyone's day.

- **Gracias** (Gra-si-as): Thank you! A magic phrase that always comes in handy.
- **¿Dónde está el baño?** (Don-de es-ta el ban-yo): Where is the bathroom? Trust us, this one's a lifesaver!

Language Schools or Resources: Where Learning Feels Like a Fiesta

Guadalajara Language Center: This location is like a linguistic festival, with competent instructors that make studying Spanish a breeze. They've got classes for every level, from total beginners to proficient speakers.

Online Resources: Can't make it to a real school? No problemo! There are loads of online tools like Duolingo, Babbel, and Memrise that'll have you parlando Español in no time.

Language Exchange Meetups: Joining a language exchange club is like organizing a fiesta for your brain. You'll meet people who wish to practice English, and you can aid them with Spanish. Win-win!

Fun and Learning in Guadalajara: Workshops That'll Make You Feel Like a Pro

Alright, friends, get ready to roll up your sleeves and delve into the exciting world of seminars and courses in Guadalajara! From mastering age-old crafts to cooking up a storm and dancing like nobody's looking, this city has got it all. Let's break everything down with a dash of comedy and a whole lot of nice sentiments.

Traditional Crafts and Skills: Unleash Your Inner Artisan

Ever imagined yourself as a magician with wood or a maestro with clay? Well, in Guadalajara, you may convert those daydreams into reality!

Pottery Pandemonium: Get your hands dirty and sculpt away! Join a pottery class and make your own ceramic masterpiece. Who knows, you could just uncover your secret gift for producing gorgeous, wonky-eyed porcelain owls.

Lucha Libre Mask Making: Embrace the passion of Mexican wrestling by making your very own luchador mask. You'll leave the session feeling like a masked superhero, ready to take on the world!

Piñata Party: Channel your inner party planner and master the skill of crafting piñatas. Because let's face it, nothing screams "fiesta" like a piñata stuffed with food and surprises.

Cooking Classes: Turn Up the Heat in the Kitchen

Calling all foodies and aspiring cooks! Guadalajara's culinary culture is going to become your playground.

Salsa Showdown: No, not the sort you dip your chips in! Learn the art of producing delectable salsas from scratch. From mild to hot, you'll create the ideal salsa for every occasion.

Tortilla Triumph: Ever tried making tortillas from scratch? It's a game-changer! Join a culinary lesson and amaze your buddies back home with your improved tortilla-flipping talents.

Margarita Mixology: Become a margarita master! Learn the secrets of producing the perfect margarita, since every excellent dinner deserves a fantastic beverage.

Dance & Music Lessons: Move and Groove Like a Local

Prepare to dance like nobody's looking and compose music like you're the next great thing!

Salsa Sensation: Put on your dance shoes and sway to the beats of salsa. Whether you're a novice or a seasoned dancer, these courses will have you rocking and grooving in no time.

Mariachi Magic: Ever fantasized of playing a guitar while shouting out soulful tunes? Join a mariachi class and let the music flow through you like tequila on a Friday night.

Folkloric Fiesta: Dive into the realm of traditional Mexican dancing. From the vibrant Jarabe Tapatío to the beautiful Danza de los Viejitos, you'll be whirling and stomping with the best of them.

Guadalajara's Fiesta Extravaganza: Where Every Day is a Celebration!

Alright, party folks, get ready to put on your dance shoes and release your inner fiesta enthusiast because in Guadalajara, the fun never stops! This city knows how to throw a fiesta that'll have you dancing until the sun comes up.

Overview of Major Festivals: Let the Good Times Roll!

International Mariachi Festival (Festival Internacional del Mariachi y la Charrería): If music is your jam, then this event is your utopia. Imagine an entire week devoted to the soul-stirring strains of Mariachi music. It's like a musical rollercoaster that'll have you singing and swaying along.

Guadalajara International Film Festival (Festival Internacional de Cine de Guadalajara): Calling all cinephiles! This festival is your golden ticket to a world of cinematic delights. From thought-provoking documentaries to heart-pounding thrillers, it's a celluloid wonderland.

Day of the Dead (Día de los Muertos): This isn't just a festival; it's a celebration of life, love, and remembering. The streets come alive with vivid altars, marigolds, and the sweet perfume of sugar skulls. It's a moment to commemorate those who've departed with pleasure and appreciation.

Dates and Locations: Where the Party's At!

International Mariachi Festival: Usually held in late August or early September, you'll find the core of the action at numerous venues around Guadalajara, including the historic Teatro Degollado.

Guadalajara International Film Festival:
Lights, camera, action! This film festival
generally takes place in March at several
sites across the city, including the glittering
Cinepolis Multiplex.

Day of the Dead: Get ready for a soul-
stirring encounter on November 1st and 2nd.
The streets, cemeteries, and plazas of
Guadalajara come alive with colorful altars
and emotional festivities.

Unique Traditions: The Quirks That Make Guadalajara Special

The Charro procession: Hold on to your
sombreros for this procession is a visual
spectacle like no other. Dashing charros
(Mexican cowboys) on prancing horses,
sparkling traditional costumes, and an
irresistible enthusiasm that'll have you
cheering along.

Gigantic Alebrijes: During the Day of the Dead festivities, expect to be amazed by giant alebrijes - fanciful, magical creatures crafted of papier-mâché. They're a riot of colors and forms that'll take you to a realm of fantasy.

The Midnight Serenade: Picture this: a serenade beneath the moonlight, with Mariachi bands filling the air with heartfelt tunes. It's a custom that'll pull at your emotions and make you believe in the miracle of love.

Chapter 8: Day Trips & Excursions: Unleashing the Fun Around Guadalajara!

Alright, amigos, it's time to put on your adventurer caps because Guadalajara's environs are brimming with adventure! Whether you're like picturesque towns, natural marvels, or historical locations, we've got day adventures tha¹t'll make your heart sing and your camera roll run out of memory.

Destinations Near Guadalajara: Where Magic Awaits

Tlaquepaque: The Artistic Wonderland

Tlaquepaque is like entering into a live, breathing artwork. Cobblestone streets, colorful buildings, and artists at every corner. Get ready to be wowed with ceramics, blown glass, and handmade treasures. And yeah, don't forget to take a shot of the painting that appears to wink at you!

Tequila: Where the Spirit Comes Alive

You've heard of it, you've probably eaten it, but have you seen where it all begins? Tequila, the home of the world-famous drink, is calling your name. Tour distilleries, drink on the good stuff, and bathe in the agave-scented air.

Chapala: Lakeside Serenity

If peaceful and tranquil is your vibe, Chapala's got it in spades. This lakeside village is all about leisurely strolls, calm boat excursions, and some of the finest fish tacos you'll ever eat. It's like a postcard comes to life!

Transportation Options for Day Trips: Getting There in Style

Choo-Choo Train to Tequila All aboard the Tequila Express! This isn't your regular train excursion; it's a party on wheels. Live music, tequila samples, and stunning landscape. It's the type of train experience you'll be talking about for years!

Private Driver for Tlaquepaque
For those who like the royal treatment, a private driver is the way to go. Sit back, relax, and let someone else manage the roads while you take in the vistas. Plus, you'll have the liberty to explore at your own speed.

Go Local with a Bus Ride
Want to genuinely see Guadalajara like a local? Hop aboard a local bus! It's not only a form of transportation; it's a cultural experience. Strike up a discussion with the

individual next to you and who knows, you could just meet a new buddy!

Recommended Itineraries: Making the Most of Your Day

Artsy Adventure at Tlaquepaque
- Morning: Dive into artisan workshops and take in the creative atmosphere.
- Lunch: Indulge in real Mexican food at a delightful neighborhood café.
- Afternoon: Stroll around galleries and don't forget to pick up a few mementos!
- Evening: Savor a leisurely supper as mariachis serenade you.

Tequila Tasting Extravaganza
- Morning: Tour distilleries and observe the tequila-making process.
- Lunch: Enjoy a great lunch with tequila-infused delicacies.
- Afternoon: Explore the agave fields and take some Insta-worthy images.

- Evening: Wrap out the day with a tequila-fueled dance party!

Lakeside Chill in Chapala
- Morning: Take a leisurely boat ride on the lake and bask in the scenery.
- Lunch: Dive into a dish of freshly caught fish tacos beside the sea.
- Afternoon: Explore the picturesque town and maybe get an ice cream cone.
- Evening: Witness a spectacular sunset across the lake before going back.

Safety Tips: Where Fun Meets Safety

Alright, fellow explorers, let's discuss safety! Guadalajara is all about having a party, but it's equally crucial to keep things safe and sound. Here are some recommendations that'll have you enjoying this bustling city worry-free!

General Safety Advice: Navigating Guadalajara like a Pro

1. Buddy System, Activate!: Traveling with friends? Stick together like peanut butter and jelly. It's not only more fun; it's safer too!

2. Stash that Passport!: Your passport is your golden ticket, so keep it locked up tight. Use the hotel safe or a concealed compartment in your suitcase. Just don't leave it sitting around like yesterday's taco.

3. Street Smarts: Watch out for those cobblestone streets! They've got character, although they may be a touch slippery. So, put on your walking shoes and take it easy.

4. Nighttime Ninja Moves: Going out after dark? Stick to well-lit locations and avoid alleys that might be harboring surprises. Remember, we're here for a good time, not a ninja showdown.

5. Hydrate Like a Pro: Mexico's got some scorching salsas, but don't let that be the only thing lighting your tongue on fire. Stay hydrated, and have agua on hand like it's your companion.

6. Cha-Ching Safety: Cash is king, but too much of it may be a problem. Use cards wherever you can, and retain a little cash for those delightful street vendors and taco booths.

Chapter 9: More Pro Tips to keep you Safe

Emergency Contacts: Your Safety Squad

1. Medical Marvels - 911: Feeling under the weather or in need of some superhuman medical attention? Dial 911, and the medics will arrive to your aid quicker than you can say "¡Ayuda!"

2. Guadalajara Tourist Police - +52 33 3818 2200: These individuals are like the protectors of the city. If you're in a pickle, they'll swoop in and rescue the day. Give 'em a call if you need a helpful hand.

3. Fire Brigade - 911: If things become a touch too caliente, and you need the fire brigade, simply phone up those trusty three numbers. They'll arrive on the scene quicker than you can say "agua, por favor!"

4. Embassy Contact: If you're an overseas traveler and find yourself in a jam, your embassy is your go-to. They've got your back, so be sure to keep their contact data ready.

Guadalajara's Healthy Hubs: Where Care Comes with a Dash of Cheer

Hospitals and Clinics: Where Healing Meets Hilarity

Alright, let's speak about the health scenario in Guadalajara, because believe me, it's not your usual hospital drama. In this city, even a trip to the doctor seems like a mini-adventure!

Sanatorio Santa Maria: If hospitals had a red carpet, Santa Maria would be rolling it out. With state-of-the-art facilities and a staff that's so nice, you'll forget you're in a hospital.

Hospital Mexico Americano: This establishment is like the Disneyland of healthcare. The physicians are like friendly magicians, and the nurses are your loyal sidekicks, making sure you leave feeling better and happier.

Centro Medico Puerta de Hierro: You know you're in excellent hands when the hospital seems like a luxury resort. Puerta de Hierro is where top-notch medical treatment meets a touch of elegance.

Pharmacies and Medical Services: More Smiles, Less Stress

Now, let's speak about pharmacies - since acquiring your medications should be a snap, not a drag!

Farmacias Guadalajara: This establishment is like the Beyoncé of pharmacies. It's got everything you need, and the staff? They're like your own cheerleaders, ready to help with a grin.

Similares: Need a prescription filled, but don't want to break the bank? Similares has got your back. It's like the budget-friendly superhero of pharmacies.

Home Health Care Services: Who says buying medical supplies has to be a chore? These men provide everything you need directly to your house, with a touch of cheerful humor.

A Healthy Dose of Guadalajara Charm

In Guadalajara, even the health scene comes with a touch of enchantment. From hospitals that seem like luxury hotels to pharmacies that treat you like royalty, your health trip here is guaranteed to be a memorable one. So, rest easy knowing that in Guadalajara, your well-being is in the hands of some of the kindest persons

Chapter 10: Staying Connected in Guadalajara: SIM Cards, Wi-Fi, and Communication Shenanigans

Hey there, tech-savvy traveler! Ready to explore Guadalajara while remaining connected? Don't sweat about losing contact with the world; we've got you covered with all the juicy facts on SIM cards, internet connection, and Wi-Fi availability in this dynamic Mexican city!

The SIM Card Shuffle

Alright, let's get into the SIM card tale.
Getting your hands on a local SIM card is as
straightforward as buying a margarita at a
beach bar. Head to any of the countless
kiosks or businesses across the city, and
you'll discover a choice of selections from
different suppliers.

Pro Tip: Telcel and Movistar are two
prominent participants in the Mexican
telecom game. They provide good coverage
and data options that'll keep your Instagram
tales flowing.

Data Plans Galore

Once you've acquired your SIM card, it's
essential to pick a data package that matches
your digital lifestyle. Whether you're a
casual surfer or a dedicated Netflix binger,

there's a strategy for everyone. Don't be reluctant to ask the pleasant shop workers for ideas - they've got the dirt on all the data bargains.

Wi-Fi Wonderland: Where to Find Your Digital Oasis

Coffee Shops: The Unofficial Remote Office

Need to send a few emails or catch up on some work? Guadalajara's coffee shop scene has your back. Not only do they dish you a delicious cup of java, but they also provide Wi-Fi speeds that'll make your laptop purr with ecstasy.

Hot Tip: Check out locations like Avila Café or Piggy Back Café for a nice area with fantastic Wi-Fi.

Parks: Nature and Net Neutrality

Yes, you read it correctly! Guadalajara's parks aren't only for picnics; they're also hotspots for free public Wi-Fi. So, why not enjoy the sun while streaming your favorite songs or video-calling your pals back home?

Insider Info: Parque Morelos and Parque Agua Azul are two of the city's finest Wi-Fi-equipped green spots.

Co-Working Spaces: Where Work Meets Play

If you're in need of a dedicated workstation, you're in luck! Guadalajara features a thriving co-working sector. These venues are not only equipped with lightning-fast internet but also provide a community of like-minded professionals.

Bonus: It's a terrific chance to meet locals and other tourists while getting your job done.

Conclusion: Where Every Corner Holds a Fiesta!

Alright, amigos, it's time for a brief summary of our excursion through the colorful streets of Guadalajara. If this city were a party, it would be the sort where you never want to leave!

From the heart-pounding sounds of Mariachi music to the mind-boggling murals that decorate the city's walls, Guadalajara is a cultural kaleidoscope that'll have you clicking images at every step. And let's not forget Tlaquepaque - those cobblestone streets are like a trip back in time, where every corner uncovers a treasure trove of artisan items.

Now, let's speak about the true stars of the show - the food! We're talking about Birria so soft it virtually melts in your tongue, Tortas Ahogadas that are so messy, you'll need a bib and a battle plan, and Pozole that's like a warm embrace from your beloved granny.

But wait, there's more! The restaurants here are like theatre, where every dish gets a standing ovation. La Chata takes tradition into the contemporary world, Hueso transforms dining into an art display, and Karne Garibaldi? Well, let's just say you won't be waiting long for your dinner!

And don't even get us started on the street food. Elotes and Esquites? It's like a carnival in your mouth! Tacos al Pastor? They're a taste fiesta! And churros and champurrado? It's like dessert nirvana on every corner.

So, my fellow travellers, as you finish up your stay in this amazing city, remember this: Guadalajara isn't just a location, it's an experience. It's a city that'll wrap its arms around you and make you feel like you've discovered a second home.

So go out, explore every corner and cranny, and take up every last drop of Guadalajara's charm. And who knows, maybe you'll leave a piece of your heart behind, waiting for your return.

Maps

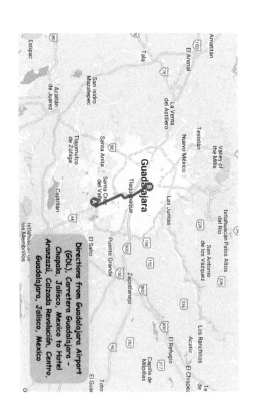

Directions from Guadalajara Airport (GDL), Carretera Guadalajara - Chapala, Jalisco, Mexico to Hotel Aranzazú, Calzada Revolución, Centro, Guadalajara, Jalisco, Mexico

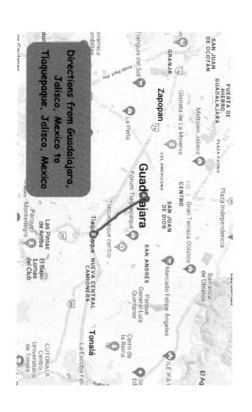

Directions from Guadalajara, Jalisco, Mexico to Tlaquepaque, Jalisco, Mexico

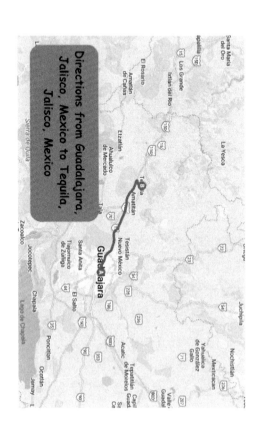

Directions from Guadalajara, Jalisco, Mexico to Tequila, Jalisco, Mexico

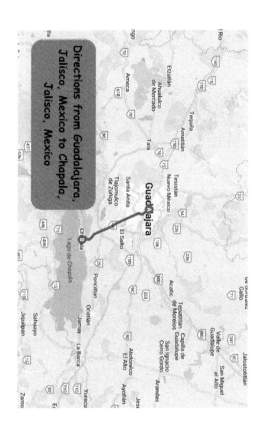

Directions from Guadalajara, Jalisco, Mexico to Chapala, Jalisco, Mexico

84

Printed in Great Britain
by Amazon

33177248R00050